Teen Smoking and Tobacco Use

A Hot Issue

Barbara Moe

 Enslow Publishers, Inc.

40 Industrial Road	PO Box 38
Box 398	Aldershot
Berkeley Heights, NJ 07922	Hants GU12 6BP
USA	UK

http://www.enslow.com

Library of Congress Cataloging-in-Publication Data

Moe, Barbara A.
    Teen smoking and tobacco use : a hot issue / Barbara Moe.
       p. cm. — (Hot issues)
    Includes bibliographical references and index.
    Summary: Describes why teens smoke, the dangers of all types
of tobacco use, and ways to quit the habit.
    ISBN 0-7660-1359-6
    1. Teenagers—Tobacco use—Juvenile literature. 2. Tobacco
habit—Juvenile literature. 3. Smoking—Juvenile literature.
[1. Smoking. 2. Tobacco habit.]
    I. Title. II. Series.
HV5745.M63 2000

                              99-050268

Printed in the United States of America

10 9 8 7 6 5 4 3 2 1

To Our Readers:
All Internet addresses in this book were active and appropriate when we
went to press. Any comments or suggestions can be sent by e-mail to
Comments@enslow.com or to the address on the back cover.

Illustration Credits: American Cancer Society, pp. 20, 36, 38, 47;
Centers for Disease Control, p. 4; Centers for Disease
Control/James Gathany, p. 52; Corbis Digital Stock, pp. 1, 12;
Image Courtesy of State of Health Products, www.buttout.com, p.
41; Trampling Tobacco Project—Alaska Native Health Board, p. 16.

Cover Illustration: Corbis Digital Stock

Contents

"In 14 years of modeling,
this is my favorite shot of myself."

Christy Turlington considers quitting smoking her biggest success.
One of her biggest regrets was that she ever started.

CDC

*T*eens often think that most celebrities use tobacco. However, many models, actors, and sports figures recognize tobacco as a health threat and choose not to use it.

Chapter 1

Who Smokes? And When Do They Start?

He is handsome, he is young, and he is brave. And he smokes! He is Jack Dawson, played by Leonardo DiCaprio in the movie *Titanic*. No one knows exactly how much influence movies have on cigarette smoking in young people, but media influences do play a part. A team of researchers looked into the question: Do movie stars encourage adolescents to start smoking? Their study concluded that "stars who smoke on and off [the] screen may encourage youth[s] to smoke."[1]

Other Influences

In addition to influence from the media—movies and television, newspapers and magazines, radio and advertising displays—pressure from friends can also cause teens to start smoking. According to a study by Min Q. Wang, Ph.D., of the Health Studies Program at the University of Alabama, the smoking behavior of best friends was the strongest predictor of smoking for both males and females in the fourteen-to-eighteen-year-old group.[2]

Although many kids try smoking, many do not

continue to use tobacco. Some only smoke a cigarette on special occasions. But young people tend to underestimate the addictive nature of nicotine, the drug in tobacco and tobacco products.

Estimates of the numbers of young people who experiment with smoking range from 47 percent to 90 percent. During the experimental phase, those who try more than three cigarettes have the highest likelihood of becoming regular smokers.[3] By age thirteen, approximately one fourth of all young people in the United States have experimented with cigarettes.[4]

Shaylah, a teen, explains how she got started:

I was about fourteen. I went to a movie with friends from school. They weren't really good friends. In fact, my other friends and I considered them "bad girls." We bought a pack of cigarettes at a little store. At the theater we didn't get caught. Maybe not getting caught reinforced the idea of trying it later again. I felt kind of juvenile sneaking cigarettes in a movie theater parking lot. To tell the truth, I felt silly. On the other hand, for a moment, the cigarette made me feel older and more mature. Like "I can do something grown-ups do."[5]

Zach, also a teenager, started smoking when he was very young.

The first time I smoked I was about eight years old. My best friend and I used to sneak his mom's menthol cigarettes and hide out in their garage to smoke. We knew how from watching his parents and other people. We got away with it the first time, which added to the excitement. The second time, his mom caught us, and we got in big trouble. My parents don't smoke, and they hate the fact that I do. It's one reason I think rebellion was such a strong aspect for me.[6]

Smoking Is a Hot Topic

In 1964, the surgeon general first pointed out some of the health hazards of smoking. Since then, the number of adult smokers has decreased.[7] However, the number of high school students using tobacco has increased. A 1997 study of more than sixteen thousand students in the United States found that 42.7 percent of the students had used cigarettes, cigars, or chewing tobacco in the thirty days prior to the study. Cigarette smoking had increased from 27.5 percent of students in 1991 to 36.4 percent in 1997.[8] Each day six thousand kids in the United States try smoking, and three thousand get hooked and become regular smokers.[9] At least 4.5 million teens in the United States between the ages of twelve and seventeen smoke cigarettes.[10]

Who Is a Regular Smoker?

Psychopharmacology, a medical journal, defines a regular smoker as a person who smokes more than five cigarettes a day. A regular smoker may also smoke every day after school (or work) but not on weekends, or may smoke every weekend but not on weekdays. Those who smoke fewer than five cigarettes a day or who do not smoke on a regular schedule are called light or occasional smokers.[11]

Brittany, a young smoker, says,

> I smoked for a while—three or four cigarettes on most days. But it always felt kind of nasty. Afterward I had to go brush my teeth. Finally I said to myself, "What in the heck am I doing this for? I have enough bad habits." So I quit. It was really that easy for me. I wonder why. I think partly because I like to hike and climb and smoking doesn't fit with that image.[12]

During her smoking days, Brittany was a light smoker. Among adults, this group makes up only about 10 percent of smokers. Light smokers have a higher success rate in quitting than heavy smokers. More kids than adults fall into the light-smoking category. But these occasional or light smokers may be at an early stage that will eventually lead to heavier smoking.[13] There is no way to predict which smokers will become addicted.

Shaylah, quoted earlier, adds: "If you're one of those types who can smoke one cigarette a day and hold on to a pack for three weeks, great. But there aren't many people like that. A smoker is a smoker is a smoker. Even a person who has one a day is a smoker. I can say that now that I've quit."[14]

Who Smokes More?

Both males and females smoke, but male students are more likely than females to report tobacco use of all kinds. In its 1997 Youth Risk Behavior Survey, the Centers for Disease Control and Prevention stated that 48.2 percent of males and 36 percent of females reported tobacco use.[15] Also, males are much more likely to use smokeless tobacco and to smoke cigars.[16]

Researchers found that high school students tended to overestimate the amount of peer smoking. They thought that double the number of people smoked than actually did. This belief that "everyone is doing it" may lead to even more smoking.[17]

However, recent studies have shown that tobacco use among girls is increasing faster than among boys, and that females often have a harder time giving up tobacco than males.[18] There has been no proven reason for this. Some researchers suggest that girls may have more symptoms of depression. Smoking is one of the ways some people try to cope with sad feelings.[19] Also, girls may start to smoke because they think smoking will keep them from gaining weight. A study by researchers at the University of Minnesota showed that girls in grades seven through ten who were worried about their weight started smoking at higher rates than nondieters and those with fewer weight concerns. Young men did not show the same weight concerns.[20]

Racial and Ethnic Differences

Smoking rates for high school students in all major racial and ethnic groups have shown recent increases. Among white students, cigarette smoking

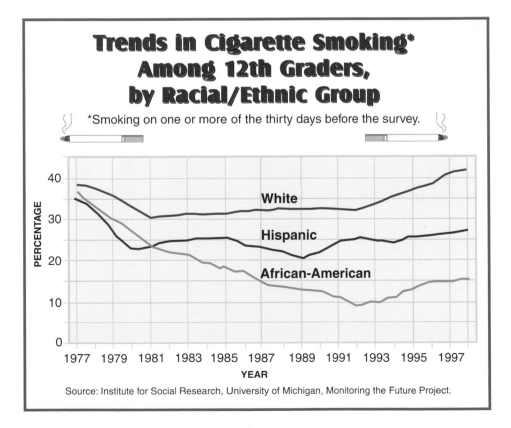

Trends in Cigarette Smoking*
Among 12th Graders,
by Racial/Ethnic Group

*Smoking on one or more of the thirty days before the survey.

Source: Institute for Social Research, University of Michigan, Monitoring the Future Project.

increased from 30.9 percent in 1991 to 39.7 percent in 1997. Among Hispanic students, cigarette smoking increased from 25.3 percent in 1991 to 34 percent in 1997. Current cigarette smoking rates increased for African-American students from 12.6 percent in 1991 to 22.7 percent in 1997.[21]

From 1980 until 1997, African-American students led other racial and ethnic groups in declining smoking rates. Daily smoking among African-American teens dropped between 1980 and 1993 but had gone up again by 1997.[22]

Sooner or Later?

The age when teens begin smoking has dropped in the past forty years. Young people are starting to use tobacco products earlier than in the recent past.[23]

Gilbey was already smoking by age six. His foster mother found a cigarette lighter in his bedroom. "Gilbey," she said, "what are you doing with a lighter?"

"It's for my cigarettes," said Gilbey.

"Cigarettes?" His foster mother tried not to let her voice show how shocked she felt. "Cigarettes aren't good for you," she said.

"I know." Gilbey looked at his feet. "I'm trying to quit. But I smoke lights."[24]

According to research, the earlier young people begin smoking, the more cigarettes they will smoke as adults and the more they will suffer from smoking-related illnesses.[25]

A person who reaches age eighteen without starting to use tobacco products is probably not going to start using them as an adult. Of adults who smoke, 88 percent began smoking cigarettes before the age of eighteen.[26]

Chapter 2

What People Smoke, Sniff, Dip, and Chew

Tobacco is a plant that is used all over the world. People smoke it, chew it, dip it, and sniff it. What happens when a product containing tobacco, such as a cigarette, is smoked? According to the American Cancer Society, "Cigarette smoking is drawing smoke, fire, and toxic substances into the lungs for the purpose of giving the body a dose of nicotine, a highly toxic and addictive drug."[1]

Nicotine is tobacco's most powerful poison. When inhaled, it travels in seconds from the lungs to the blood to the brain.[2] When tobacco is chewed or sniffed, nicotine travels from the membranes of the mouth or nose to the brain.

Cigarettes

In addition to nicotine, cigarette smokers end up with by-products such as tars, gases, and many other chemicals known to cause or suspected of causing cancer in their bodies. The American Lung Association provides a list of these chemicals and how various industries use them.[3] Smokers might want to ask themselves: Would I want these chemicals in my house or garage—or in my lungs?

Tars and gases cause lung damage. Tars are chemical particles that condense as thick, adhesive substances. When people inhale smoke from burning tobacco, tar accumulates in the lungs, causing smoker's cough, breathing problems, and sometimes cancer.[4]

Burning tobacco produces harmful gases, including hydrogen cyanide, nitrogen oxide, ammonia, and carbon monoxide. Carbon monoxide (CO) is a dangerous gas that can kill people. When produced by smoking, carbon monoxide binds much more strongly than oxygen with the hemoglobin in the red blood cells. Hemoglobin is the substance in

*S*moking cigarettes can be a very filthy habit. Cigarette butts can get all over the place and cigarette smoke can get absorbed into clothes and furniture.

a person's blood that helps carry oxygen to various body parts, including the brain. By taking up space in the red blood cells, carbon monoxide prevents adequate delivery of oxygen to body tissues, causing damage to the heart and blood vessels.[5]

In combination with nicotine, carbon monoxide is doubly dangerous. Not only does carbon monoxide displace the oxygen in a person's red blood cells, but nicotine stimulates the heart, causing it to beat faster, increasing its need for oxygen.[6]

Many smokers of light or ultra-light cigarettes expect to reduce smoking risks with these choices. Few realize that lights and ultra-lights deliver the same amount of tar to the body as a regular cigarette.[7] An article in the *Journal of the American Medical Association* calls low-tar, low-nicotine cigarettes a "scam" by the tobacco industry.[8] When smoking such cigarettes, smokers tend to "compensate." They may inhale more deeply with one cigarette, or they may smoke two cigarettes in rapid succession.[9]

Cigars

In the past, it was fathers or grandfathers who smoked cigars, often to celebrate special events like the births of their children and grandchildren. But now, many teens are smoking them, too. In 1996, the Robert Wood Johnson Foundation surveyed students in 202 high schools throughout the United States. This study showed that 6 million students had smoked a cigar in the previous year. Males, cigarette smokers, and smokeless tobacco users smoked the most cigars.[10]

According to *The New England Journal of Medicine*, cigar sales in the United States increased

Beware of Bidis

The New York Times has reported a recent fad among teen smokers—a type of cigarette called a bidi. Bidis are thin, sweet-tasting cigarettes that are imported from India. The tobacco in bidis is wrapped in a leaf, so that the cigarettes resemble a marijuana joint.

Many teens think that bidis are not as bad for the body as regular cigarettes since they are so small and seem more natural. However, the State Department of Public Health states that in one bidi there could be as much as five times the tar and triple the amount of nicotine than in a regular cigarette. That would make bidis a lot more damaging and addictive than regular cigarettes.

This has many people worried, since bidis seem to appeal to teens. Teens like them because they come in different flavors and are often cheaper than cigarettes. This appeal combined with their greater health risks and potential for addiction makes bidis another deadly product that teens should steer clear of.

Source: Carey Goldberg, "Study Details Smoking Fad Among Youth," *The New York Times*, September 17, 1999, p. A12.

nearly 50 percent between 1993 and 1997. The upward trend is largely the result of occasional cigar smoking by middle-aged and younger men, but cigar smoking is also increasing in teenagers and women.[11]

Many people believe cigars are safer than

cigarettes because the smoke is usually not inhaled. Cigars, however, contain between 10 and 444 milligrams of nicotine. A person can take an hour to smoke a big cigar, which may contain as much tobacco as a pack of cigarettes.[12] Cigar smoking can cause cancers of the oral cavity, larynx, esophagus, and lung.[13]

Smokeless Tobacco

Smokeless tobacco includes chewing tobacco and oral and nasal snuff. Manufacturers produce different styles of smokeless tobacco, such as loose leaf, plug, and twist tobacco. Oral snuff, sometimes called dip, is made of fine-grained tobacco with added flavoring. Users dip a pinch of loose snuff or use a packet of snuff which resembles a small tea bag. They put the tobacco in their cheek, under their tongue, or between their bottom teeth and lower lip. Tobacco used in the mouth is sometimes called spit tobacco.

Nasal snuff is a finely ground tobacco that is inhaled into the nostrils. This form of tobacco, however, is rarely used today.

In the past thirty years, more teens have started using smokeless tobacco. The Centers for Disease Control and Prevention report that white male students are the largest group of smokeless tobacco users.[14]

Some young people like smokeless tobacco because they can use it without detection. There is no smoke, no smell, and they can tuck small amounts in various parts of the mouth. But smokeless tobacco is just as addictive as other tobacco products and equally dangerous. Users get gray or yellowish teeth, red and receding gums, and

*E*ven though a chewing tobacco user may think he or she looks cool, to anyone else the habit is disgusting.

precancerous sores in their mouths. Eventually, smokeless tobacco users may get cancers of the mouth, throat, esophagus, and pancreas. Their habit may lead to stomach ulcers, high blood pressure, heart disease, strokes, and even death.[15]

"Smokeless" does not mean "smoke less." The bodies of people who use these products absorb a great deal of nicotine, which may cause as much damage to the body as smoking cigarettes. In addition, studies show that when people try to give up smokeless tobacco, they sometimes switch to cigarettes.[16]

Damien, a smoker, talks about his use of tobacco:

> I've tried to quit smoking a bunch of times. I started using tobacco at age nine. A friend's dad had taken the wrong lunch, and the kid had his dad's lunch with a pack of Marlboro Reds in the box. So we smoked a few. I quit when I was sixteen; at the time I was chewing, too. I had been a dedicated hockey player from the age of seven. Smoking didn't go with hockey, but chewing seemed okay. I started smoking again at a party when I was nineteen, and I was still chewing. At age twenty, I stopped chewing, but I've been smoking ever since.[17]

Chapter 3

Getting Ready to Resist

Most young people do not use tobacco. Of those who do, many say they wish they had known beforehand why some teens try that first cigarette or first pinch of dip. Caitlyn started smoking at age fourteen and quit at eighteen. It is obvious, she says, that if you do not start smoking, you will not have to stop.

> Don't start for the fun of it. My friends and I started smoking without knowing we were walking into a trap. Don't ignore the facts. Talk to people who smoke or people who have quit. Ask them, "If you could do it all over again, would you smoke?" You might hear a hundred percent of them saying that if they could do it all over again, they *wouldn't* smoke.[1]

Saying No

Saying no to using tobacco takes planning. "Just try it once," someone is sure to say. How does a person respond?

There are many different ideas that have helped young people avoid that first cigarette.

Keeping busy. Boredom is one of the main reasons teens start to use tobacco. Those who are involved in after-school activities are likely to hang out with other busy people who are not interested in smoking or chewing tobacco.

Making exercise a part of every day. Getting some kind of vigorous exercise each day can be part of the plan to keep busy and healthy. Some people do the same kind of exercise each day. Others like to vary their routines. The important thing is to do something.

Finding a sense of belonging. A sense of belonging to a group is important to everyone. When teens smoke, they find this sense of community with their smoking buddies. Caitlyn, a former smoker, says, "Before I quit it seemed to me smokers had more fun. Often outside, the smokers were laughing and talking while inside the nonsmokers were looking bored. Even when it was twenty degrees outside, the smokers were out there sharing a bond."[2]

However, it is possible to get the same feeling of belonging without smoking cigarettes.

Avoiding alcohol. Alcohol decreases inhibitions and weakens a person's resolve not to smoke or chew tobacco.[3] For many people, alcohol and cigarettes seem to make a great team. Actually, though, alcohol adds to the harmful effects of nicotine.[4] People who want to say no to tobacco should also say no to alcohol.

Considering costs. Before smoking that first cigarette, young people might want to ask themselves if they can afford such an expensive habit. At current prices, a pack-a-day smoker will spend approximately $1,200 a year on cigarettes. There may be other costs as well, such as smoking-related health costs or missing work or school.

Self-esteem. People with high self-esteem—a belief in one's self and one's worth—may be less likely to use tobacco than those people with low self-esteem. High self-esteem makes a person less of a follower and more of a leader, and more able to resist pressure to use tobacco. Also, someone who has a good self-image is less likely to equate self-worth with looks or popularity, or to turn to smoking as a way to try to look cool. Those who have high self-esteem know they are okay just as they are.

Young people who do not have high self-esteem can work at getting it. They can give themselves

*M*ore and more restaurants are adopting a "no smoking" policy. Some states have even made laws against smoking in restaurants or public buildings.

messages such as "I deserve a healthy lifestyle" or "I am a strong person without tobacco."

Making a decision not to use tobacco products can go a long way toward increasing self-esteem. The decision not to smoke or dip is a vote for a healthy body—a vote for a person who deserves to be fit.

Why Do Young People Start Using Tobacco?

Why do teens and even younger children start to use tobacco? The list is a long one and includes the belief that smoking or dipping looks cool, that nicotine relieves stress, and that smoking keeps people thin. Other reasons include advertising, other media messages, the influence of family and friends, and the desire to live for the moment.[5]

Advertising. Most young people do not mention advertising to explain why they started using tobacco products. But most experts believe advertising plays a large part in teen smoking.

Some formerly famous advertising symbols such as Joe Camel are gone. His creator, the R. J. Reynolds Company, "voluntarily" killed him on July 9, 1998, partially in response to critics who said he had too much influence on kids. According to Stephanie Stapleton in *American Medical News*, before Joe "died," evidence surfaced showing that tobacco companies had deliberately targeted young people to receive their cigarette advertising messages.[6]

The messages tobacco companies would like young people to receive include ideas such as: Tobacco use is relaxing and sociable, tobacco use is part of becoming an adult, and tobacco use is not

Famous People Who Died From a Tobacco-Related Illness

Name	Occupation	Died of . . .
John Candy	actor, comedian	heart attack
Ty Cobb	baseball player	cancer, diabetes, chronic heart disease
Walt Disney	animator, producer	lung cancer (acute circulatory collapse following operation to remove a tumor)
Sigmund Freud	psychologist	cancer of the jaw
Ulysses S. Grant	Civil War general; United States president	throat cancer
Groucho Marx	actor, entertainer	lung cancer
David McLean	actor, model; former TV "Marlboro Man"	lung cancer
R. J. Reynolds	founder of R. J. Reynolds Tobacco Company	emphysema
Babe Ruth	baseball player	oral cancer
Frank Sinatra	singer	heart attack
Ed Sullivan	entertainer	lung cancer

Source: "A Few of Our Losses," *Quitsmokingsupport.Com*, n.d., <http://www.quitsmokingsupport.com/noteables.htm> (November 16, 1999); © Gene Borio, the Tobacco BBS.

only safe but also healthy and glamorous, something successful people do.[7] These statements, of course, are all false.

The models who pose for cigarette advertisements look handsome or beautiful, have fun, and are athletic and slim. But if those models smoked in real life, their teeth would probably not stay white. If they continued to smoke, telltale creases would likely form around their lips. Even David McLean, the actor who originally posed as the seemingly strong and tough Marlboro Man in magazine ads, died of lung cancer from smoking cigarettes.

Tobacco companies target young people because it is their business. Every day approximately thirty-five hundred Americans quit smoking, and an additional twelve hundred tobacco customers die of smoking-related illnesses. Those figures add up. Tobacco companies need to recruit five thousand new smokers every day (about 2 million a year) to maintain their customer base and profit margins.[8]

Other media influences. Teenagers and young adults make up a large segment of the moviegoing public. That is why antismoking organizations, such as the American Lung Association, want to see less smoking in movies. Stanton A. Glantz, professor of medicine at the University of California, found that 57 percent of lead movie characters smoked in contrast to 24 percent of today's "real" American adults.[9]

Even in films depicting the past, reality may get distorted. For example, in the movie *Titanic*, two young lovers light up at the dinner table even though few women smoked in 1912. According to actual

Titanic reports, female passengers argued over men's smoking in the lifeboats.[10]

Family and friends. According to Action for Smoking and Health (ASH), children with family members who smoke are twice as likely to smoke as those who do not have these influences.[11] Some young people who grow up with tobacco products in the home may have easy access to them. If those around them use tobacco, it may seem natural for them to use tobacco, too.

But easy access does not mean a teen will eventually smoke or chew. Nathan, a young antismoker, says, "Even when we were little, my younger brother and I did everything we could to get our mom to stop smoking. One time we pooled our

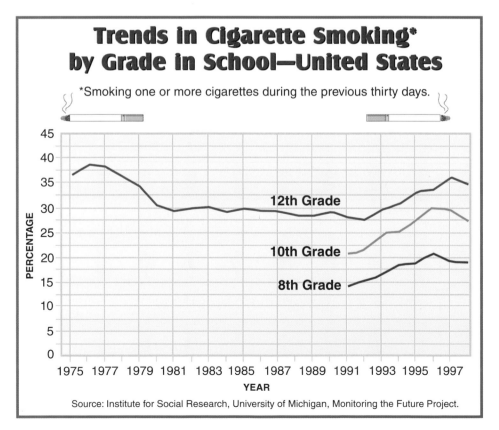

Trends in Cigarette Smoking*
by Grade in School—United States

*Smoking one or more cigarettes during the previous thirty days.

12th Grade

10th Grade

8th Grade

Source: Institute for Social Research, University of Michigan, Monitoring the Future Project.

cash and bought her some fancy filters. She thanked us; she said she would try them. But a couple of days later, she said they ruined the taste of the cigarette, and she threw them away. There's no way I would ever smoke after living for eighteen years with her addiction."[12]

Living for today. To some teens smoking seems like fun. It appears to enhance pleasure and it seems exciting. It gives people the sense of living on the edge. Most young people cannot climb Mount Everest. What can they do that is risky? They can use tobacco. Researchers studied young people in fourth grade through high school. They found that at all grade levels, smokers were more likely than non-smokers to engage in risk-taking behaviors and to report more stress and depression.[13]

The teen years are supposed to be exciting, the best years of a person's life. However, a teen can have fun without risking his or her life by smoking.

Caitlyn, quoted earlier, reflects back on her days as a smoker: "I associated smoking with great times. I can remember experiencing a beautiful spring morning with a friend. The sun shone on the melting snow. We listened to the drips, admired the green around us, and said goodbye to winter. I imagined I was enjoying the moment partly *because* of the cigarette. After I quit, I compared a similar moment, and it was just as beautiful without the smoke."[14]

Chapter 4

Why People Stay Hooked

People who smoke or chew tobacco often become addicted to nicotine—a drug found in tobacco. Addictive substances, such as nicotine, are very difficult to give up.

Nicotine is much more addictive than people think. Although current smokers realize a lifetime of smoking is dangerous, they do not expect to find themselves in that category. According to a report of the surgeon general of the United States, most seniors in high school who smoked predicted they would not be smoking cigarettes five years in the future. However, at follow-up five years later, of those who smoked one pack or more a day, only 13 percent had quit. Seventy percent still smoked one pack or more per day.[1]

Olivia, an older woman and ex-smoker, says, "An addiction is a powerful thing. Addicted people don't care who they hurt—they'll sacrifice themselves, their parents, their kids. They'll hurt anyone to get what they need. I know; I've been there."[2]

What Is Addiction?

The World Health Organization (WHO) defines addiction as a pattern of behavior in which the use of a substance causes a person to value that use more than other behaviors that were formerly important.[3] When a person has an addiction to a tobacco product, the desire for nicotine begins to control many of the person's thoughts and behaviors. The person cannot stop using tobacco just because he or she wants to.

Who Gets Addicted?

Anyone can get addicted to nicotine. However, a person's genes (hereditary units) can make some people more prone to nicotine addiction. One study of male twins published in the *New England Journal of Medicine* showed that identical twins are more likely to have similar smoking behaviors than fraternal twins.[4]

Scientists suggest that some people have a biochemical switch that opens up a reward channel in the brain after only a few exposures to a certain substance.[5] When these people experience stress, for example, they may be more vulnerable to nicotine addiction than others. Over time, the brain needs more and more of the substance (in this case, nicotine) to reproduce the original effect. The brain of an addicted person functions normally only when the substance is present. As the time between cigarettes (or smokeless tobacco) gets longer, the smoker experiences withdrawal symptoms such as irritability.[6]

Andrea talks about her craving for nicotine: "When I turned eighteen and moved out, I used to go over to my parents' house for Sunday dinner.

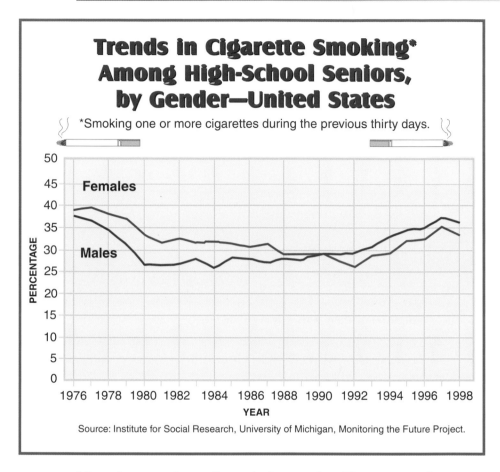

Trends in Cigarette Smoking*
Among High-School Seniors,
by Gender—United States

*Smoking one or more cigarettes during the previous thirty days.

PERCENTAGE

Females

Males

YEAR

Source: Institute for Social Research, University of Michigan, Monitoring the Future Project.

After about an hour, I needed a smoke. They wanted me to stay longer. But they wouldn't let anyone smoke in their house, and they would have hit the ceiling if I said I had to go outside for a cigarette break. So I made up excuses—somewhere I had to go. Then, as soon as my car door closed, I lit up."[7]

The "When" of Addiction

For people addicted to nicotine or other drugs, the pathway of need gets more deeply ingrained with each use. The longer a person uses tobacco, the harder it gets to quit. The person associates "cues," such as a smoky room, their car, certain friends, talking on the telephone, or sipping drinks, such as coffee or alcohol, with nicotine. These cues act as triggers for tobacco use.[8]

Five Stages of Nicotine Addiction

Nicotine addiction develops in five stages:

1. Preparatory Stage—A person gains knowledge and forms beliefs (true or false) about tobacco use.

2. Initial Trying Stage—A person tries tobacco two or three times.

3. Experimentation—A person repeatedly uses tobacco at irregular intervals over an extended period or uses tobacco during certain situations, such as parties.

4. Regular Smoking—A person establishes a pattern of tobacco use, such as every day after school or every weekend.

5. Addiction—A person uses tobacco every day with an internal "need" or craving.[9]

Withdrawal

One of the main reasons people keep smoking (or chewing or dipping) has less to do with the pleasure of tobacco use than the discomfort of quitting. Whether tobacco users quit suddenly or gradually, they will experience symptoms caused by the withdrawal of nicotine from their bodies. They become more anxious, restless, and impatient. Because of this they will find it harder to get to sleep, despite feeling tired most of the time. People who are trying to quit tobacco will also become irritable and find it harder to concentrate. They will experience constipation, dizziness, headaches, heart palpitations, and increased hunger and perspiration. Of course, along with all these symptoms comes a strong desire to use tobacco.

These symptoms are the worst in the first twenty-four to forty-eight hours. They diminish in intensity over a period of weeks. However, a craving for nicotine may last for months or even years.[10]

Andrea adds,

> At age sixteen, I began smoking almost daily. By age eighteen, I was addicted to nicotine. I think that between the ages of sixteen and eighteen,

Nicotine Withdrawal Symptoms

✓ Anxiety

✓ Craving sweets

✓ Craving tobacco

✓ Constipation or diarrhea

✓ Depression

✓ Falling blood pressure

✓ Falling heart rate

✓ Fatigue, drowsiness, and insomnia

✓ Headache

✓ Increased hunger and calorie intake

✓ Irritability

✓ Lack of concentration

✓ Nausea

Source: "Nicotine Withdrawal Symptoms," *Quitsmokingsupport.Com*, n.d., <http://www.quitsmokingsupport.com/new.htm> (November 16, 1999).

there was a window of opportunity for me to say, "I don't need this," and get off nicotine. I knew I was addicted at eighteen because when my parents let me use their car, I'd smoke it up even though that was against the rules. I was ashamed of myself. But, more importantly I began to get an idea of the seriousness of this addiction. I'd throw whole packs [of cigarettes] out the window. The very next day I'd find myself mooching cigarettes from friends or buying my own. As you can see, it wasn't long after I became addicted that I wanted to quit. But I'm still smoking.[11]

A study reported in the *Journal of the American Medical Association* discussed the strong desire people have for certain drugs. Those who had used several drugs, including nicotine, said that their desire for nicotine when it was unavailable was as high or higher than their desire for heroin, alcohol, or cocaine.[12]

Not All Bad?

Some people argue that the effects of nicotine are not all bad and may even be helpful in the short term.[13] Nicotine can improve concentration, alertness, dexterity, and memory. Nicotine also temporarily helps lift feelings of depression in some people. A person could argue that nicotine increases productivity. But in an increasingly smoke-free environment, if a person loses time in smoking areas and takes time off because of respiratory illnesses, a decrease in productivity actually occurs.

When Andrea (quoted earlier) was eighteen, she tried to quit smoking. On her first nonsmoking day, she noted, "So far today I'm doing well. I've already discovered I can get more stuff done when I'm not always running outside to take a smoke break."[14]

Physical and Psychological Dependence

In addition to physical dependence, or addiction, the use of tobacco products also causes psychological dependence.[15] Some people call cigarettes their friends. They feel cigarettes have some positive qualities: They are always available, they do not complain or demand a response as human friends do, and they do not need special care or consideration.

Andrea adds, "I'm trying to quit, and I think I'm going to make it. It's very hard for me to quit because cigarettes have been a comfort to me, my little buddies. Smoking seemed to help when I was lonely or needed to focus."[16]

People who are dealing with psychological withdrawal issues will probably ask themselves the following questions:

➤ If I do not smoke, what do I do with my hands?

➤ How will I keep my mouth busy?

➤ If I am trying not to smoke, how can I go to places in which I have always smoked before?

➤ If I do not smoke, how will I deal with stress?

➤ What about friends? If I give up smoking, will I have to give up my friends who still smoke?

It seems like different young people have different ideas about quitting smoking. Chuck, a young ex-smoker, says, "It doesn't bother me to be around people who smoke (unless I'm with lots of smokers in an enclosed space). How could I find fault? I used to be smoking with them."[17]

"Since I've quit, I don't want to be around smokers, but if I really like certain people, I'm not going to walk away from them just because they smoke," Caitlyn says, "But I have to think of myself, and I know there is no 'finish line' with addiction. So it's hard to say if I could handle spending a lot of time with smokers."[18]

"I don't know about being friends with smokers," Shaylah comments, "People's behavior does change. Maybe I could be a positive influence on someone. I already have set an example for several of my friends who quit after I did."[19]

Chapter 5

The Effects of Tobacco Use

Would you play with a loaded gun? Most people would say no. Yet those who use tobacco products are doing something similar every time they smoke or chew. Cigarettes kill more Americans each year than AIDS, alcohol, car accidents, fires, illegal drugs, murders, and suicides combined.[1] Cigarette smoking causes at least one of every five deaths in the United States.[2] If present trends continue over the next forty years, the number of deaths worldwide from tobacco use will increase from 3 million each year to 10 million each year.[3]

Inside the Body: Organ Damage

What are the effects of tobacco on the individual parts of the body? The negative results of smoking (some irreversible) begin almost immediately. According to the American Council on Science and Health, smoking for as short a time as five years damages almost every organ in the human body.[4] Smoking can be a slow death.

Lung Damage

The respiratory tract is one of the first places in the body to show damage. This damage is especially harmful to athletes. Even young smokers have more trouble "catching their breath" than nonsmokers. Teens who smoke may not notice early changes and may not realize that tobacco use is affecting their health. Even if they know the health risks, they think they can slide for many years without problems.

Respiratory problems occur because tobacco destroys the cilia (small hairs) that line the respiratory tract.[5] Mucus accumulates in smokers' throats. They have a "goopy" cough, and they tend to get more colds than their nonsmoking friends.

Shaylah, quoted earlier, tells what smoking did to her: "I smoked for a few years with no problems. Then one winter I got a terrible lung infection. The doctors discovered I was only breathing at 20 percent of my lung capacity. When my doctor told me that, I freaked out. It scared the you-know-what out of me. Have you ever seen a picture of a smoker's lungs—all black and gross? It's scary and on top of that, mine were infected."[6]

Identical twins Beccah, a smoker, and Karen, a nonsmoker, learned firsthand about the early effects of smoking. As part of a study, the eighteen-year-old girls volunteered for testing at Lutheran Medical Center in Denver, Colorado. In one test, doctors used an infrared camera to measure the teenagers' body temperatures. Both girls immersed one hand in a bucket of ice, which caused their temperatures to drop. As soon as Karen pulled her hand from the ice, the camera recorded that her hand immediately returned to its normal temperature. Beccah's hand

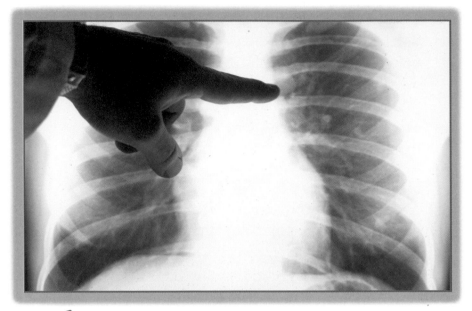

*A*n x-ray can show a doctor whether or not a person's lungs have been damaged by smoking.

stayed cold much longer, indicating some circulatory dysfunction.

In another test, the twins worked out on treadmills. During the exercise, Karen's heart pumped at a lower, healthier rate than did Beccah's. A pulmonary-function test showed that Beccah could not exhale as hard or as fast as Karen, the nonsmoker.[7]

"When you can't breathe, nothing else matters" is the motto of the American Lung Association.

After years of smoking, older people often develop emphysema, a disease in which the air space of the lungs becomes overinflated and nonelastic. Smokers sacrifice lung flexibility, which is necessary for normal breathing. Smoking may also cause bronchitis, asthma, and allergic reactions.[8]

Cancer

According to the American Cancer Society, cancer develops when something such as smoking damages the body's genetic code of normal cells and breaks down the body's natural protection against cancer. The damaged cells reproduce quickly; they form clumps of cells called tumors. Tumors steal nutrition and energy from the rest of the body. They may spread and grow large enough to block vital body functions. Unless something stops the abnormal growth, cancer kills.

The American Cancer Society reports that tobacco use is now linked not only to cancers of the lung but also to cancers of the mouth, pharynx, larynx, esophagus, pancreas, uterine cervix, kidney, and urinary bladder.

A 1997 study by the National Cancer Institute showed that 75 percent of former smokers had damaged deoxyribonucleic acid (DNA). DNA is the carrier of genetic information in the body's cells; damaged DNA may predispose a person to cancer. Only 3 percent of nonsmokers had damaged DNA.[9]

Other Damage from Tobacco

Cancer is not the only negative effect of tobacco use. Tobacco also affects the bones. Smoking contributes to osteoporosis, a condition of brittle bones, which usually affects older women.[10]

The digestive system can also be affected. Use of tobacco products can cause stomach ulcers.[11]

The eyes and ears can be affected as well. Smoking increases the risk of eye disease, including cataracts, a condition in which the lens of the eye loses transparency.[12] Smoking may also cause premature hearing loss in some people.[13]

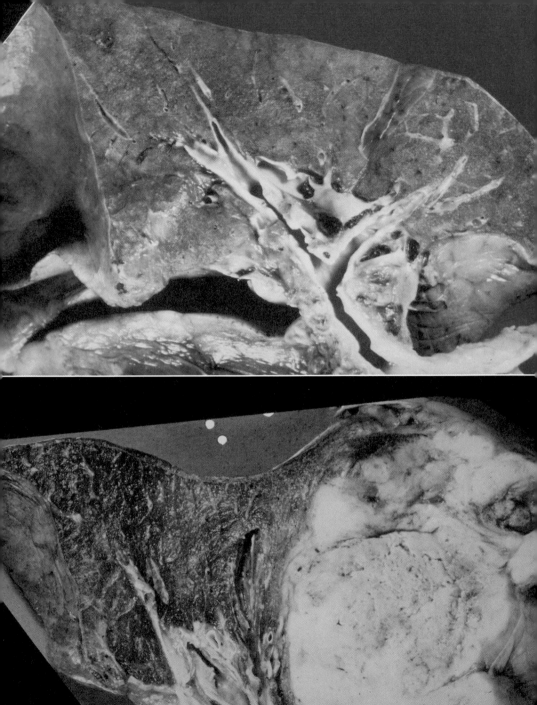

A smoking habit will continually destroy a healthy lung (top) until it is blackened and cancerous (bottom).

Stained teeth and gum disease with subsequent tooth loss are also part of the picture for users of tobacco products. Even the skin takes a hit from smoking. Lines in the face, especially around the mouth, are a smoker's hallmark.

Tobacco smoke also damages blood vessels, impedes blood circulation to various body parts, and can lead to coronary heart disease. Tobacco can activate the blood platelets and make them stick together, increasing the possibility of strokes. Smoking doubles the risk of strokes in both men and women. Women who smoke and take birth control pills have ten times more risk of stroke than non-smoking women.

Smoking and Pregnancy

Many teens do not spend a lot of time thinking about becoming parents. But smoking has several harmful effects on babies—even before they are born. In fact, parental smoking may cause infertility problems. Couples in which even one person smokes are at least three times more likely to have infertility problems as couples in which neither partner smokes. Women who smoke have more miscarriages than those who do not. Men who smoke have fewer and more abnormal sperm cells than nonsmoking men.[14]

Babies born to mothers who smoke tend to be smaller than other babies, are more likely to have malformations, are more likely to be born early, and are sometimes stillborn (born dead).[15] Recent studies show that babies born to women who smoke may not be as smart as other babies.[16] Worst of all, some scientists say that pregnant smokers can pass a cancer-causing substance derived from nicotine to their unborn babies.[17]

More Problems

Tobacco use affects a person's looks, body, relationships, and the health of others around him or her.

Smoking may strain family relationships as parents object to their children's tobacco use. Cigarette smoking is often a warning of other problems. For example, teens who smoke are three times as likely to use alcohol, eight times as likely to use marijuana, and twenty times as likely to use cocaine.

Social problems also include days lost from work or school and the costs involved in treating sick smokers.[18] Tobacco costs money that a person could be spending on healthy activities or saving for the future.

Smoking may also cause the loss of friendships.

Young Smokers Tend to Have

✓ lower levels of school achievement than nonsmokers

✓ fewer skills to resist pressures to smoke

✓ friends who use tobacco

✓ lower self-images than nonsmokers

✓ the intention to quit school

✓ a parent, parents, or siblings who use tobacco

✓ lack of involvement in athletics

✓ positive attitudes toward tobacco advertising and tobacco use

✓ anxiety or depression

Sources: Centers for Disease Control and Prevention. "Preventing Tobacco Use Among Young People: A Report of the Surgeon General." Washington, D.C.: U.S. Government Printing Office, 1994; Barbara S. Lynch and Richard J. Bonnie, eds., *Growing Up Tobacco Free: Preventing Nicotine Addiction in Children and Youths* (Washington D.C.: National Academy Press, 1994), pp. 52–56.

*T*his poster conveys why a lot of people do not like to date smokers.

Some people decide they do not want to hang around smokers for their own health.

Tobacco use may cause the loss of dating opportunities. Some people do not like kissing smokers or someone who has a wad of chewing tobacco in his or her mouth. Ex-smokers and nonsmokers often cannot stand the smell of smoke. Some smokers become ashamed or secretive about their habit. Andrea describes what happened to her one summer:

At my summer job in this law firm I had my eye on a cute dark-haired fellow intern named Joe. I'd never smoked around him, and I was hoping he'd ask me out. One day, Joe put his face close to mine and said, "Andrea, are you a smoker?" He has nerve, I thought. I quickly answered no. My next thought? He knows. And now he knows I'm a liar, too. After this incident, I couldn't even make eye contact with Joe. I still hoped he would ask me out, but he never did.[19]

Secondhand Smoke

Most people who smoke know that cigarettes are harmful, but they decide to take the risk. People who do not smoke may feel comfortable about their decision to avoid nicotine's powerful poison. But they may also want to consider the effects of secondhand smoke.

There are two kinds of secondhand smoke. Mainstream smoke is exhaled into the air by the smoker. Even more dangerous is sidestream smoke, which goes directly into the air from the burning tobacco product. Sidestream smoke has higher concentrations of poisons than mainstream smoke. Most of the smoke in a roomful of smokers is sidestream smoke. Breathing this air is sometimes called passive or involuntary smoking.[20]

Olivia is a mother who smoked when her children were young. Her children are grown up now, and neither of her sons smokes. But she smoked when they were little and now blames herself for subjecting them to secondhand smoke. "I smoked in the house, and I smoked in the car," she says. "Back then we didn't have a clue about the dangers. We smoked at the movies and in the grocery store. After a party at my house, the air would be thick with smoke—like a battlefield. We thought people who didn't allow smoking in their houses were kooks [or people with weird ideas]."[21]

Chapter 6

Quitting Time

For most people, stopping the use of tobacco products is hard work. According to pediatrician Seth Ammerman, many tobacco "quitters" have made at least seven previous attempts to stop smoking or chewing.[1] "Cold turkey," which means using tobacco one day and then never using it again starting the following day, works for some, but most people need help and support from several sources.

Organizations such as the American Cancer Society, the American Lung Association, and the American Heart Association have suggested smoking-cessation ideas that have worked for many people. Smokers who are trying to quit may want to take some of these ideas and add their own to make an individualized quitting plan.

Getting Ready to Quit

Many people who have stopped using tobacco products did so

1. by setting a "quit date" not too far in the future and sticking to it. The Great American

Smokeout is always the third Thursday of November and World No-Tobacco Day is May 31. But people who want to stop tobacco use can set their own quitting day

2. by making an announcement of the quit date to family and friends

3. by asking their smoking or chewing friends not to use tobacco around them

4. by trying to find someone to quit with but not waiting for such a person to appear

5. by buying the supplies needed to keep their mouth "busy"—hard candy, raw veggies and apples, air-popped popcorn, sugarless gum, toothpicks

6. by observing the times of day they have been most tempted to use tobacco, then planning ways to change their behavior at those times

7. by making an action plan for getting through the first day and by thinking of supports for their new nonsmoking behavior. What will they do when the first craving hits? The second? The third? Quitting "cold turkey" does not mean quitting without support

8. by thinking of ways to reward themselves after the first successful day and by thinking of other ways to use the money they will save when they are not buying tobacco products, like going to the movies or buying new compact discs

Some Changes Ex-Smokers May Notice

✓They get rich. (Well, maybe not rich, but a pack-a-day former smoker is likely to save $1,200 a year.)

✓Their breath smells good; their hair smells good; their fingers smell good; their clothes smell good; they smell good.

✓They wake up without mucus in their throat.

✓Their goopy cough disappears.

✓They do not get as many colds as they did when they smoked.

✓They are able to run faster and for a longer time and do not get as winded.

✓They regain control of their lives.

9. by thinking of what they might do if they are not successful on their first attempt at quitting

10. by learning the usual withdrawal symptoms and realizing that these will decrease after the first twenty-four to forty-eight hours[2]

Quitting Day and After

Along with quitting comes the need to maintain nonsmoking behavior. This can be very hard. But, if a person uses certain strategies, he or she can stay tobacco-free forever.

Planning ahead. Throw away all tobacco-related materials—cigarettes, cigars, smokeless tobacco, matches, lighters, ashtrays. Do not buy more of these things or borrow them from friends. Anticipate stressful days and realize that everyone has them. By knowing that other people can handle stress without nicotine, former tobacco users realize they can, too.

Keeping the body busy. A smoker's hands are used to holding a cigarette. So if the hands are kept busy, they will not miss holding a cigarette. They can be kept busy by fixing things around the house, doing yard work, cooking for the family, organizing a room, or brushing the dog.

Keep the body itself in action. Exercise is one key to a tobacco-free person's success. Exercise helps fight the depressed feelings that may have kept some people smoking or chewing. Walking, jogging, bicycling, playing tennis, soccer, football, or basketball are only a few of the many ways the body can keep busy.

It is important to stay active in a healthy atmosphere. Hang out with tobacco-free friends. Go to places where smoking is not allowed, such as to a department store, movie theater, nonsmoking restaurant, library, or museum.

Healthy eating, drinking, and breathing. Eat three healthy meals (or several smaller meals) every day and make them last as long as possible. This can be done by chewing food thoroughly and remembering there is no need to race to a post-dinner cigarette. After the meal, have a cup of herbal tea or a hard candy to substitute for the post-dinner cigarette.

Drink lots of fluids. Water, juices, herbal teas, and caffeine-free soft drinks help rid the body of nicotine. Caffeine increases the urge to smoke, so it is good to avoid coffee and other drinks containing caffeine. Alcohol should also be avoided since it

*A*lcohol abuse often increases tobacco use. A person trying to quit using tobacco should avoid alcohol, because alcohol use decreases a person's resistance to nicotine.

lowers the body's defenses and breaks down willpower.

When the craving for nicotine hits, take deep breaths and count to fifteen. By breathing in and out slowly, the body will inhale clean air. After this exercise is done, drink an eight-ounce glass of water. The craving for nicotine should have subsided.

Visualizing. When tempted to use tobacco, one can also think of negative images, such as blackened lungs or yellow teeth. Even better, get a picture of those images from a magazine or your family doctor and keep it in your room. This will be a reminder of tobacco's dangerous effects. Think of smoker's breath and how quitting will eliminate it.

Attitude Adjustment and New Routines. Try to give up old routines and do not stop at former smoking "haunts." Those who get the urge to smoke after a meal might try going for a walk after dinner.

A positive attitude is important. Remember, each day that one does not use tobacco is a successful day, and that failing is not the end of the world, but simply a chance to try again.

Try starting a journal and record your successes, as well as stresses. By recording feelings and the ways they cope, "quitters" will have provided themselves with interesting reading material for the weeks and months ahead. It also helps for a person to begin considering him or herself tobacco-free.

Rewards. By saving the money not spent on tobacco products, ex-users are giving themselves a reward. For example, a former pack-a-day smoker who does not smoke for six months will be able to save about six hundred dollars. One can also treat each day being tobacco-free as a reward in itself.

Quitting Methods

There are many different ways to quit using tobacco. Different methods work for different people. If one wants to quit tobacco he or she has to find the method that is most comfortable.

Cold turkey. Drug addicts coined the term "cold turkey" when, after quitting the use of drugs, they got goose pimples, hot and cold flashes, and flu-like discomfort. In recent years, people have used the expression to describe the sudden withdrawal from any type of activity. Those who quit tobacco cold turkey should prepare themselves for a few days of feeling like a piece of cold, skin-puckered turkey meat. Cold turkey is one way to stop using cigarettes

Chronology of Health Improvements After Quitting Smoking

The American Cancer Society presents the following table of health benefits that begin twenty minutes after a person stops smoking. These benefits continue for up to fifteen years.

Twenty minutes later
✓ Blood pressure begins to drop
✓ Temperature of hands and feet returns to normal

Eight hours after quitting
✓ Carbon monoxide and oxygen levels in the blood return to normal

Twenty-four hours after quitting
✓ Chance of heart attack decreases

Forty-eight hours after quitting
✓ Ability to taste and smell improves

Two weeks to three months after quitting
✓ Circulation of blood improves
✓ Walking gets easier
✓ Lung functioning may increase as much as 30 percent

One to nine months after quitting
✓ Overall energy increases
✓ Coughing, sinus congestion, tiredness, and shortness of breath decrease
✓ Movement of cilia, which help keep the lungs clean, returns to normal

One year after quitting
✓ Risk of coronary heart disease decreases to half of that for a smoker

Five years after quitting
✓ Risk of cancer of the mouth, throat, and esophagus is half that for a smoker
✓ Risk of having a stroke is reduced to that of a nonsmoker (This may take up to fifteen years)

Ten years after quitting
✓ Lung cancer death rate decreases to half the risk for a continuing smoker
✓ Risk of cancer of the mouth, throat, esophagus, urinary bladder, kidney, and pancreas decreases even more

Fifteen years after quitting
✓ Risk of coronary heart disease decreases to that of a nonsmoker

Source: American Cancer Society brochure, *The Health Benefits of Smoking Cessation*, Centers for Disease Control and Prevention, DHHS Publication No. (CDC) 90-8416, 1990.

or chewing tobacco. Giving up tobacco cold turkey means using it one day and not using it the next—or any time in the future. Quitting cold turkey does not necessarily mean going it alone or on pure willpower. A person can quit cold turkey and still get the help of a counselor or a support group.[3]

Tapering off. The process of gradually cutting down the "dose" of nicotine that enters the body is called tapering off. Rosemary was able to quit by tapering off.

> First I cut out the cigarette I had in the morning—the minute my feet hit the floor. Some time after that, I was able to quit going outside to smoke at work in the middle of the morning. Then I cut out the after-lunch cigarette. Not long after that, my mid-afternoon cigarette started making me feel sick. I kept at the process of cutting back for several months until I was able to eliminate that final cigarette.[4]

Some people, however, do not have the willpower to quit by tapering off.

Nicotine Replacement Therapy. The users of nicotine replacement therapy (NRT) face a two-step quitting process. First they stop using nicotine in the usual ways (smoking, chewing, or dipping tobacco) and substitute transdermal (skin) patches, nicotine gum, nasal spray, or a nicotine inhaler to deliver a dose of nicotine to the body. Some of these products are available over-the-counter; others require a doctor's prescription.

The second phase of quitting involves a gradual tapering off from the nicotine replacement. When people stop using NRT, withdrawal symptoms still occur, though they are less severe than with cigarettes or chewing tobacco.[5] For example, chewing gum containing nicotine is less addictive and less harmful than smoking because the gum contains less nicotine and eliminates the harmful chemicals of tobacco.

For most people, the whole process takes about three months, although some people continue to use these "helpers" for a longer time. For specific advice on how long to use a medication, a person should consult package directions or a health care provider. However, the person who is quitting should remember that nicotine is a dangerous poison in any form.[6]

Non-nicotine medication. Dr. Allan V. Prochazka and fellow researchers suggest that anxiety and stress play a role in preventing people from quitting the use of tobacco products. They showed that anti-depressants can help some people quit smoking.[7] Zyban is the name for a non-nicotine medication that has helped many people quit. Tobacco users let this medication build up in their bloodstream a week before their quit date. Although bupropion hydrochloride, the main ingredient in Zyban, has been used for many years to treat depression, the medication seems to work well for smoking cessation even in those who do not feel depressed. There is a small risk of seizure when using Zyban, and those with eating disorders and seizure disorders should not use it at all.[8]

Complementary or Alternative Help. In addition to the smoking cessation therapies described above, some people try complementary or alternative therapies. The two most common are acupuncture and hypnosis.[9]

The most common type of acupuncture used for smoking cessation involves the placement of a small, semipermanent needle into an acupuncture point on the ear. When they feel a craving, patients press the ear. The aim is to promote the release of endorphins and overcome withdrawal symptoms.[10] Hypnosis may take place in one session, several sessions, or in a group session. In any case it seems to work best in people who are highly motivated to take responsibility for their own behavior.[11]

Physicians, Support Groups, and Other Help. Some doctors counsel young people about the hazards of tobacco or give them advice about quitting. One such doctor is Eric France, a pediatrician with Kaiser Permanente in Denver, Colorado. He begins with parents and their young children. "For example, a mom brings her four-year-old son in with a cough," says Dr. France. "I listen to Johnny's chest. After that, I may ask him, 'Do you smoke?' Johnny may laugh, but say, 'No, but Mommy does.'" During

*T*his graveyard, which is next to a tobacco field, is a grim reminder of the substance's danger to the body's health.

the visit, Dr. France tries to find out how much motivation the mother has to stop smoking. He hopes to empower her to quit. He offers resources and support. At the same time, Johnny is listening and will hopefully learn about the dangers of smoking early on.

When Dr. France works with young people over the age of eleven or twelve, he always asks about friends. He agrees with other experts that friends play a critical role in smoking initiation. "Prevention is the key," he adds. After explaining the process of physiological nicotine addiction, Dr. France asks young smokers to consider quitting while there is still time—before they get "hooked."[12]

Support groups refer to any helping network. An informal support group may consist of friends and family. A formal support group, such as the American Lung Association's Freedom from Smoking® group program, offers seven sessions to help people set up and follow their Quit Smoking Action Plan.

In many communities, Nicotine Anonymous offers a twelve-step program for quitting tobacco use. Twelve-step programs employ the principles of Alcoholics Anonymous, in which a person admits to powerlessness over a substance and seeks support in recovery from its use.

Some hospitals and health plans offer support groups. These support groups usually are four to seven sessions, lasting one or two hours each session.[13]

Having a Relapse

For those who do not quit the first time they try (or even the second or third time), all is not lost. Dennis

C. Daley, author of *Kicking Addictive Habits Once and For All*, says that a return to a former addictive habit may be just a "slip" or a "lapse" rather than a full-blown relapse. A lapse may make people realize their vulnerability to the addictive behavior and may actually strengthen a person's resolve to keep trying.

Most important, tobacco users need to remember not to get mad at themselves. Each attempt at quitting is a positive step toward the ultimate goal.

Those who have lapses (or relapses) may want to try:

> ➢ different techniques from the ones used previously. For example, after a relapse, a person who has tried to quit "cold turkey" might use nicotine-replacement therapy

> ➢ writing in a journal at the beginning and end of each day focusing on expectations and results

> ➢ creating a helping network of family and friends and being sure to ask them for support

> ➢ making an "action plan," a pledge to keep going even when the going gets tough.[14]

When it comes to quitting the use of tobacco products, no single "cure" fits all. For most people, a habit so easy to start is extremely difficult to get rid of. Each person must design, or get help in designing, his or her own quitting strategy. The biggest help is the determination of the tobacco user to quit.

Organizations

American Lung Association
1740 Broadway
New York, NY 10019
(800) LUNG-USA
<http://www.lungusa.org>

National Center for Tobacco-Free Kids
1707 L Street NW, Suite 800
Washington, DC 20036
(202) 296-5469
<http://www.tobaccofreekids.org/>

Nicotine Anonymous
P.O. Box 591777
San Francisco, CA 94159
(415) 750-0328
<http://www.nicotine-anonymous.org/>

Stop Teenage Addiction to Tobacco (STAT)
Northeastern University
360 Huntington Avenue
241 Cushing Hall
Boston, MA 02115
(617) 373-7828
<http://www.stat.org/>

Internet Addresses

CDC's Tips: Tobacco Information and Prevention Source
<http://www.cdc.gov/tobacco>

Children Opposed to Smoking Tobacco (C.O.S.T.)
<http://www.costkids.org>

Kickbutt.org: A Service of Washington "Doc"
<http://www.kickbutt.org>

No Smoke Home Page
<http://www.smokefreekids.com>

The Quitnet
<http://www.quitnet.org>

Smokescreen Action Network
<http://www.smokescreen.org>

Chapter 1. Who Smokes? And When Do They Start?

1. Janet M. Distefan, B.A., et al., "Do Movie Stars Encourage Adolescents to Start Smoking? Evidence from California," *Preventive Medicine*, vol. 28, January 1999, pp. 1–11.

2. Min Q. Wang, et al., "Family and Peer Influences on Smoking Behavior Among American Adolescents: An Age Trend," *Journal of Adolescent Health*, vol. 16, March 1995, pp. 200–203.

3. M.A.H. Russell, "The Nicotine Addiction Trap: A 40–Year Sentence for Four Cigarettes," *British Journal of Addiction*, vol. 85, 1990, pp. 293–300.

4. Eliseo J. Perez-Stable, M.D., and Elena Fuentes-Afflick, M.D., "Role of Clinicians in Cigarette Smoking Prevention," *Western Journal of Medicine*, vol. 169, July 1998, p. 23.

5. Personal interview with Shaylah, Denver, Colorado, December 14, 1998.

6. Personal interview with Zach, Denver, Colorado, November 27, 1998.

7. Centers for Disease Control and Prevention, "Cigarette Smoking Among Adults—United States, 1991," *Morbidity and Mortality Weekly Report*, vol. 42, no. 12, April 2, 1993, pp. 230–233; John P. Pierce, et al, "Has the California Tobacco Control Program Reduced Smoking?" *Journal of the American Medical Association*, vol. 280, September 9, 1998, p. 893.

8. Centers for Disease Control and Prevention, "Tobacco Use Among High School Students—United States, 1997," *Morbidity and Mortality Weekly Report 1998*, April 3, 1998, vol. 47, p. 229; *Journal of the American Medical Association*, April 22/29, 1998, vol. 279, p. 1250.

9. John P. Pierce, Ph.D., et al., "Trends in Cigarette Smoking in the United States: Projections to the Year 2000," *Journal of the American Medical Association*, vol. 261, January 6, 1989, pp. 61–65.

10. Centers for Disease Control and Prevention in *The Wall Street Journal*, October 9, 1998, p. A4 (W), p. B9 (C), col. 5.

11. Saul Shiffman, "Tobacco 'Chippers,'—Individual Differences in Tobacco Dependence," *Psychopharmacology*, vol. 97, 1989, pp. 539–547.

12. Personal interview with Brittany Sullivan, Denver, Colorado, November 2, 1998.

13. Barbara S. Lynch and Richard J. Bonnie, eds., *Growing Up Tobacco Free: Preventing Nicotine Addiction in Children and Youths* (Washington, D.C.: National Academy Press, 1994), p. 37.

14. Personal interview with Shaylah, Denver, Colorado, December 14, 1998.

15. *Journal of the American Medical Association*, April 22/29, 1998, vol. 279, p. 1250.

16. Centers for Disease Control and Prevention, "Cigar Smoking Among Teenagers—United States, Massachusetts and New York, 1996," *Morbidity and Mortality Weekly Report*, May 23, 1997, vol. 46, no. 20, pp. 433–440; Centers for Disease Control and Prevention, "Tobacco Use and Usual Source of Cigarettes Among High School Students—United States, 1995," *Morbidity and Mortality Weekly Report*, May 24, 1996, vol. 45, no. 20, pp. 413–418.

17. Howard Leventhal, et al., "Is the Smoking Decision an 'Informed Choice'? Effect of Smoking Risk Factors on Smoking Beliefs," *Journal of the American Medical Association*, vol. 257, June 26, 1987, pp. 3373–3376.

18. Seth Ammerman, M.D., "Helping Kids Kick Butts," *Contemporary Pediatrics*, vol. 15, February 1998, p. 64.

19. Neal L. Rojas, et al., "Nicotine Dependence Among Adolescent Smokers," *Archives of Pediatrics and Adolescent Medicine*, vol. 152, February 1998, p. 151; Susan Flagg Godbey and Rachelle Vander Schaaf, "Sad Habit," *Prevention*, vol. 49, August 1997, p. 40.

20. Simone A. French, Ph.D., et al., "Weight Concerns, Dieting Behavior, and Smoking Initiation Among Adolescents: A Prospective Study," *American Journal of Public Health*, vol. 84, November 1994, pp. 1818–1820.

21. *Journal of the American Medical Association*, April 22/29, 1998, vol. 279, p. 1250.

22. Perez-Stable and Fuentes-Afflick, p. 24.

23. Patricia F. Coogan, ScD, et al., "Factors Associated with Smoking Among Children and Adolescents in Connecticut," *American Journal of Preventive Medicine*, vol. 15, July 1998, p. 17.

24. Personal interview with Mandy Copeland, caseworker, Adoption Alliance, Aurora, Colorado, September 14, 1998.

25. L. Chassin, et al., "The Natural History of Cigarette Smoking: Predicting Young-Adult Smoking Outcomes from Adolescent Smoking Patterns," *Health Psychology*, vol. 9, 1990, pp. 701–716.

26. Centers for Disease Control and Prevention, "Preventing Tobacco Use Among Young People: A Report of the Surgeon General," Washington, D.C.: Department of Health and Human Services, 1994, p. 67.

Chapter 2. What People Smoke, Sniff, Dip, and Chew

1. *The Decision Is Yours*, American Cancer Society, Atlanta, 1996.

2. Kathiann Kowalski, "Taking Aim at Teen Smoking," *Current Health 2*, vol. 22, March 1996, p. 13.

3. "Chemicals in Cigarettes," *American Lung Association*, <http://www.lungusa.org/tobacco/smoking–factsheet.html> (August 17, 1999).

4. Donald F. Tapley, Thomas Q. Morris, Lewis Rowland, and Jonathan Lapook, eds., *The Columbia University College of Physicians and Surgeons Complete Home Medical Guide*, 3rd rev. ed. (New York: Crown Publishers, Inc., 1995), p. 125.

5. Ibid.

6. Ibid.

7. Lynn Kozlowski, et al., "Smokers Misperceptions of Light and Ultra Light Cigarettes May Keep Them Smoking," *American Journal of Preventive Medicine*, vol. 15, July 1998, p. 17.

8. Richard D. Hurt and Channing Robertson, "Prying Open the Door to the Tobacco Industry's Secrets About Nicotine: The Minnesota Tobacco Trial," *Journal of the American Medical Association*, vol. 280, October 7, 1998, p. 1177.

9. Ibid.

10. "Cigar Smoking Among Teenagers—United States, Massachusetts, and New York," *Morbidity and Mortality Weekly Report*, May 23, 1997, vol. 46, no. 20, p. 433.

11. Carlos Iribarren, et al., "Effect of Cigar Smoking on the Risk of Cardiovascular Disease, Chronic Obstructive Pulmonary Disease, and Cancer in Men," *The New England Journal of Medicine*, vol. 340, June 10, 1999, p. 1773.

12. Phil B. Fantanarosa, ed., "Questions and Answers: Nicotine Content and Health Risk of Cigars," *Journal of the American Medical Association*, vol. 276, December 18, 1996, pp. 1857–1858.

13. *Morbidity and Mortality Weekly Report*, May 23, 1997, vol. 46, no. 20, p. 433.

14. "Tobacco Use among High School Students—United States, 1997," *Journal of School Health*, vol. 68, May 1998, p. 202.

15. Neal L. Benowitz, et al., "Daily Use of Smokeless Tobacco: Systemic Effects," *Annals of Internal Medicine*, vol. 111, July 15, 1989, pp. 112–116.

16. Ibid.

17. Personal interview with Damien Sargo, Denver, Colorado, October 1, 1998.

Chapter 3. Getting Ready to Resist

1. Personal interview with Caitlyn Romberg, Denver, Colorado, November 23, 1998.

2. Ibid.

3. Michael J. Klag, ed., *Johns Hopkins Family Health Book* (New York: HarperCollins Publishers, Inc., 1999), p. 85.

4. William J. Blot, et al., "Smoking and Drinking in Relation to Oral and Pharyngeal Cancer," *Cancer Research*, vol. 48, June 1, 1988, p. 3282.

5. "Hooked on Tobacco: The Teen Epidemic," *Consumer Reports*, vol. 60, March 1995, pp. 142–147.

6. Stephanie Stapleton, "Papers Deal Another Blow to Tobacco: Youth Smoking Files Likely to Hurt Quest for Limited Liability," *American Medical News*, vol. 41, February 2, 1998, p. 1.

7. "Hooked on Tobacco: The Teen Epidemic," pp. 142–147.

8. Barbara S. Lynch and Richard J. Bonnie, eds., *Growing Up Tobacco Free: Preventing Nicotine Addiction in Children and Youths* (Washington, D.C.: National Academy Press, 1994), p. 105.

9. Sherryl Connelly, "Film Smoking Has Health Activists Fuming," *St. Louis Post-Dispatch*, July 20, 1998, p. E3.

10. Ibid.

11. "Fighting a Losing Battle," *Pediatrics for Parents*, vol. 16, April 1995, p. 7, from *ASH Smoking and Health Review*, September October, 1995.

12. Personal interview with Nathan Kight, Denver, Colorado, September 27, 1998.

13. Patricia F. Coogan, "Factors Associated With Smoking Among Children and Adolescents in Connecticut," *American Journal of Preventive Medicine*, vol. 15, July 1998, p. 17.

14. Personal interview with Caitlyn Romberg.

Chapter 4. Why People Stay Hooked

1. Centers for Disease Control and Prevention, "Preventing Tobacco Use Among Young People: A Report of the Surgeon General," Department of Health and Human Services, Atlanta, Ga., 1994, pp. 84–85.

2. Personal interview with Olivia, Denver, Colorado, December 30, 1998.

3. "Nomenclature and Classification of Drug- and Alcohol-related Problems: A Shortened Version of a WHO Memorandum," *British Journal of Addiction*, vol. 77, 1992, p. 10.

4. Dorit Carmelli, Ph.D., et al., "Genetic Influences on Smoking—A Study of Male Twins," *The New England Journal of Medicine*, vol. 327, September 17, 1992, pp. 829.

5. "Substance Dependence," *Harvard Women's Health Watch*, August 1998, p. 4.

6. Ibid.

7. Personal interview with Andrea Maxwell, Denver, Colorado, December 14, 1998.

8. "Substance Dependence," p. 4.

9. Barbara S. Lynch and Richard J. Bonnie, eds., *Growing Up Tobacco Free: Nicotine Addiction in Children and Youths* (Washington, D.C.: National Academy Press, 1994), p. 44.

10. Neal L. Rojas, et al., "Nicotine Dependence Among Adolescent Smokers," *Archives of Pediatrics & Adolescent Medicine*, vol. 152, February 1998, p. 151.

11. Personal interview with Andrea Maxwell.

12. Lynn T. Kozlowski, et al., "Comparing Tobacco Cigarette Dependence with Other Drug Dependencies: Greater or Equal 'Difficulty Quitting' and 'Urges to Use' but Less 'Pleasure' from Cigarettes," *Journal of the American Medical Association*, 261:6, February 10, 1989, pp. 898–901.

13. Peter Brimelow, "Thank You for Smoking . . . ?" *Forbes*, vol., 154, July 4, 1994, p. 80.

14. Personal interview with Andrea Maxwell.

15. Lynch and Bonnie, p. 39.

16. Personal interview with Andrea Maxwell.

17. Personal interview with Chuck Williams, Denver, Colorado, June 19, 1999.

18. Personal interview with Caitlyn Romberg, Denver, Colorado, November 23, 1998.

19. Personal interview with Shaylah, Denver, Colorado, December 14, 1998.

Chapter 5. The Effects of Tobacco Use

1. "Number of Deaths Per Year, 1990," Office on Smoking and Health, Centers for Disease Control and Prevention.

2. Centers for Disease Control and Prevention, "Cigarette Smoking—Attributable Mortality and Years of Potential Life Lost— United States, 1990," *Morbidity and Mortality Weekly Report*, August 27, 1993, pp. 645–649.

3. Richard Peto, "Smoking and Death: The Past 40 Years and the Next 40," *British Medical Journal*, vol. 309, October 8, 1994, p. 937.

4. Charles Henderson, "Some Damage Lasts After Smokers Quit," *Cancer Weekly Plus*, September 7, 1998, p. 1.

5. American Lung Association, "About Lungs and Lung Disease," April 1997, pp. 2–15.

6. Personal interview with Shaylah, Denver, Colorado, December 14, 1998.

7. Diane Eicher, "They're Identical Twins. Only One Craves Nicotine. And at 18 Her Body Already Exhibits Tell-Tale Signs of Smoking," *Denver Post Lifestyles*, March 22, 1998, p. F–1.

8. American Lung Association, "About Lungs and Lung Diseases."

9. American Cancer Society, "The Decision is Yours," 1996.

10. Alan Blum, M.D., "Beware," *Bottom Line Personal*, August 15, 1992, p. 8.

11. M. Tatsuda, et al., "Effects of Cigarette Smoking on the Location, Healing, and Recurrence of Gastric Ulcers," *Hepato-Gastroenterology*, October 1987, pp. 223–228.

12. O. Cekic, "Effect of Cigarette Smoking on Copper, Lead, and Cadmium Accumulation in Human Lens," *British Journal of Ophthalmology*, February 1998, pp. 186–188.

13. Karen J. Cruickshanks, et al., "Cigarette Smoking and Hearing Loss: The Epidemiology of Hearing Loss Study," *Journal of the American Medical Association*, vol. 279, June 3, 1998, pp. 1715.

14. Alan Blum, M.D., p. 8.

15. American Cancer Society, "Why Start Life Under a Cloud?" 1997.

16. David L. Olds, et al., "Preventing Intellectual Impairment in Children of Women Who Smoke Cigarettes During Pregnancy," *Pediatrics*, vol. 93, February 1994, p. 228.

17. Rita Rubin, "Smoking Moms' Fetuses Can Carry Carcinogen," *USA Today*, August 24, 1998, p. 1D.

18. *Facts About . . . Secondhand Smoke*, American Lung Association, Washington, D.C., January 1998, p. 1.

19. Personal interview with Andrea Maxwell, Denver, Colorado, December 14, 1998.

20. *Facts About . . . Secondhand Smoke*.

21. Personal interview with Olivia, Denver, Colorado, December 30, 1998.

Chapter 6. Quitting Time

1. Seth Ammerman, "Helping Kids Kick Butts," *Contemporary Pediatrics*, vol. 15, February 1998, p. 72.

2. Barbara S. Lynch and Richard J. Bonnie, eds., *Growing Up Tobacco Free: Preventing Nicotine Addiction in Children and Youths* (Washington, D.C.: National Academy Press, 1994), p. 33.

3. Dianne Hales and Robert E. Hales, *Caring for the Mind: The Comprehensive Guide to Mental Health* (New York: Bantam Books, 1995), p. 207.

4. Personal interview with Rosemary Zavella, Denver, Colorado, December 2, 1998.

5. Hales and Hales, p. 208.

6. Michael J. Klag, *Johns Hopkins Family Health Book* (New York: HarperCollins Publishers, 1999), p. 83.

7. Allan V. Prochazka, et al., "A Randomized Trial of Nortriptyline for Smoking Cessation," *Archives of Internal Medicine*, vol. 158, October 12, 1998, pp. 2035.

8. "Using Medications," American Lung Association® Quit Smoking Action Plan, 1998, <http://www.lungusa.org/partner/quit/step02.html> (November 1, 1999).

9. George Lewith, et al., *Complementary Medicine: An Integrated Approach* (New York: Oxford University Press, 1996), p. 227.

10. Ibid., 229.

11. Ibid., 229–230.

12. Personal interview with Eric France, pediatrician, Kaiser Permanente, Denver, Colorado, June 21, 1999.

13. "Preparing to Quit," American Lung Association® Quit Smoking Action Plan, 1998, <http://www.lungusa.org/partner/quit/step01.html> (November 1, 1999).

14. Dennis C. Daley, *Kicking Addictive Habits Once and For All: A Relapse-Prevention Guide* (Lexington, Mass.: D.C. Heath and Company, 1991), pp. 60–68, 189–190, 193.

bronchi—Breathing tubes in the chest.

bronchitis—An acute or chronic inflammation of the mucus membranes of the trachea and bronchi, involving excess mucus and a productive cough.

cancer—Abnormal growth of body cells, causing tumors or growths in various parts of the body, which may invade surrounding tissues and distant sites.

carbon monoxide—An odorless, poisonous gas produced by cigarette smoke, which decreases the ability of the blood to furnish oxygen to the body.

carcinogen—A cancer-causing substance, such as those found in tobacco.

cilia—Small hairlike projections on the surfaces of cells of the respiratory tract, which are destroyed by smoking.

circulatory system—The network of body channels carrying blood, including the heart and blood vessels.

cold turkey—Cutting off tobacco use in one step.

dipping—Putting loose tobacco (snuff) in the mouth in order to experience the effects of nicotine.

emphysema—A chronic condition in which air spaces in the lungs become overinflated and nonelastic.

mainstream smoke—Smoke exhaled into the air by the smoker.

nicotine—A powerful poison and the addicting substance in tobacco.

nicotine replacement therapy—A method that helps a person stop smoking by substituting nicotine in the form of gum, skin patches, nasal spray, or inhalation.

pulmonary function test—A measurement of lung capacity and functioning.

respiratory system—The organs of the body that help with breathing.

sidestream smoke—Smoke that goes directly into the air from the burning tobacco product.

smokeless tobacco—Includes all tobacco not smoked, such as chewing tobacco, oral snuff, and nasal snuff.

stroke—A closing up of the blood vessels to the brain, which deprives the brain of oxygen necessary for normal functioning. This is one possible result of smoking.

tar—Chemical particles that condense as sticky resins in a smoker's lungs, causing a cough, breathing problems, or cancer.

tumors—Damaged cells that can reproduce wildly in various body parts, impinging on healthy cells.

withdrawal symptoms—Uncomfortable feelings that set in when people cannot have (or choose not to have) a substance to which they have been addicted.

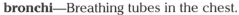

Casey, Karen. *If Only I Could Quit: Recovering from Nicotine Addiction*. Center City, Minn.: Hazelden, 1995.

Cigarettes: What the Warning Label Doesn't Tell You: The First Comprehensive Guide to the Health Consequences of Smoking. Amherst, N.Y.: Prometheus Books, 1997.

Folkers, Gladys, and Jeanne Engelmann. *Taking Charge of My Mind & Body: A Girls' Guide to Outsmarting Alcohol, Drug, Smoking, and Eating Problems*. Minneapolis, Minn.: Free Spirit Publishing, Inc., 1997.

Haughton, Emma. *Viewpoints: A Right to Smoke?* New York: Franklin Watts, 1997.

Hyde, Margaret O. *Know About Smoking*. 3rd ed. New York: Walker and Company, 1995.

Lang, Susan S., and Beth H. Marks. *Teens and Tobacco: A Fatal Attraction*. Brookfield, Conn.: Twenty-First Century Books, 1995.

Lee, Richard S., and Mary Price Lee. *Caffeine and Nicotine*. New York: The Rosen Publishing Group, 1998.

McMillan, Daniel. *Teen Smoking: Understanding the Risk*. Springfield, N.J.: Enslow Publishers, Inc., 1998.

Perry, Robert. *Focus on Nicotine and Caffeine: A Drug-Alert Book*. Brookfield, Conn.: Twenty-First Century Books, 1995.

Rustin, Terry A. *Quit and Stay Quit: A Personal Program to Stop Smoking*. Center City, Minn.: Hazelden, 1995.

Wekesser, Carol, ed. *Current Controversies: Smoking*. San Diego, Calif.: Greenhaven Press, 1996.

Index